Inside Out

*Poems From the Lives
of Five Accomplished Women*

Martha Deborah Hall

Plain View Press
P.O. 42255
Austin, TX 78704

plainviewpress.net
sb@plainviewpress.net
512-441-2452

Copyright © 2011 Martha Deborah Hall. All rights reserved under International and Pan-American Copyright Conventions. No part of this book may be reproduced or distributed in any form or by any means, or stored in a data base or retrieval system, without written permission from the author. All rights, including electronic, are reserved by the author and publisher.

ISBN: 978-1-935514-12-1
Library of Congress Number: 2010942094

Cover art: "Still life with spotted jug," 15" x 18," mixed media by
　　　　　Jenny Grevatte
Cover design by Susan Bright

Disclaimer
The poems in this book are the invention of the author and not intended to be biographical or historical presentations of the lives of these five women.

Contents

I Dorothea Dix (1802–1887) — 7

Inside Out — 9
Fodder in the Stew — 10
Don't Tell Anyone Where We Are — 11
Moving on — 1840'S — 12
The Maine of My Youth — 13
Inside Rain — 14
In the State Hospital — 15
Prettiest Apple — 16
I Want to Be ... — 17
Outside St. Shepherd's Church — 1869 — 18
Freezing — 17
My Fog Over the Harbor — 19
And Then It Rained — 21

II Margaret Bourke-White (1904–1971) — 23

Don't Touch — 25
When You and I Were Young, You... — 26
Klepto — 27
A Favorite Subject, Ralph — 28
Zoom — 29
The Wedding Ring — 30
Shoot — 31
Usa, 1930'S, Begonia — 32
Buchenwald Fairy Tale, 1945 — 33
Leipzig-Mochau, 1945 — 34
Photographing Joseph Stalin for "Life Magazine" — 35
Beyond the Glam — 36
The Jump — 37
Once Upon — 38
Mother — 39
Bourke-White at Sixtyish — 40

III Greta Garbo (1905–1990) — 41

Dear Mother, — 43
Churchill, Onassis, Garbo — 44
Abortion Hollywood Style — 45
Dear Dad, — 46
Some Coffee, a Wooden Bench — 47

Greta on Amies	48
For My Sister Alva	49
Waste Not, Want Not…	50
Would I Rather…	51
To Moje	52
I Wondered If…	53
Outside Greta's Flat	54
God Jul	55
I'm a Let-It-Snow-Again Norsewoman	56
Mata Hari	57

IV Edith Piaf (1915–1963) 59

From the Refrigerator…	61
Waiting for Her Again	62
L'argent	63
Balloons	64
Monkey-See, Monkey-Do	65
My Little Sparrow	66
Marcel, My Prizefighter	67
Hear My Song	68
Blueberry in the Needle	69
A Toast for Marguerite Monnot	70
The Piaf Prescription	71

V Carol Burnett (1933–) 73

February's Joyless Child	75
Childhood Scents	76
My Shoebox	77
On the Train	78
At the Welfare Dentist	79
Going to the Movies	80
Mom, Down the Hall Again	81
Don, You Were My…	82
"Blame It on My Youth"	83
We Were	84
On the Cover	85
Carol's Motto	86
Defense Against Being a Workaholic	87
Carrie	88
Back Home in San Antonio, Forty Years Later	89
Carol's Theory	90

About the Author	91

To Judith Devlin, another accomplished woman, I lovingly dedicate this collection

Acknowledgments

All of the Greta Garbo poems were printed in a chapbook titled, *The Garbo Reels*, published by Pudding House Publications in 2010. (ISBN 1-58998-848-5). "Seeds and Ashes" was awarded 2nd Prize in the members contest and published by the Poetry Society of New Hampshire.

1

Dorothea Dix

(1802–1887)

Inside Out

You've left me alone in the backyard, where pigeons flock, their grey babies cry. The house was void of love. Whatever you served up, I rejected. Leave me alone with Bach. Let me learn to cry by smiling. Let me magnify my goodness, be my voice, my strength. If I want to go around and around, allow me. You are the dwarves of my existence. Let me tack to the left and then to the right and finally reach the port of my self-willed destination. I can't affix my signature to a deed. You say I'm unladylike if I don't darn stockings or cook the perfect turkey. You look at me from the outside-in. Look at me from the inside-out.

Fodder in the Stew

You often know you should go, but you don't. Like a fool mom stayed, blended into the draperies, trying not to be seen, but needing *to*. Their wedding formed a theory they call shambles. Their vows, their promises, formed mud pies in the sand, covered by grey satchels loaded with quarrels. Blues flowed from every inlet. This child steadily boiled over with hatred.

Don't Tell Anyone Where We Are

I was a back-forth rubber band when they tried to take Helga away, like a head without a cap to wear, a neck without a scarf. Helga's name means holy-faithful. She is that to me. You have copper roofs with gabled ends, pink perennials in ochre pots. In my mind I see brick fireplaces with mantles made of marble. Here, mice scurry over our faces; pigeons roost and coo on nearby ledges. Rain seeps through cracks in this coal-like dank bin. Without Helga, my life would be void of love. She has a lace collar, patent shoes with strawberry bow ties in her golden hair. She's my vintage porcelain soul mate. I feel so dark within when Helga goes to sleep.

Moving on — 1840's

Here I am at grandmother's in a warm night gown with pink and white slippers to match. The wet terry cloth towel slacks on the rack. I haven't read past page one in my book. The grandfather clock I brought from home stands quite tall over in the corner as it chants 7 AM. I promised I would leave the past behind, but the clock is the symbol of the fact that I can't. It's hard to be comfortable with rocks offshore once you've stubbed your toes on them. I'm in my twentieth year. I've learned money is the phantom we believed would save us, but doesn't. I don't want to end up in an almshouse nor be drunk on money. I know I'll have to learn to crack an egg one day but right now there's no need for a wedding gown with lace cap. I don't want to be the worm that spoils the apple, nor the candy jar that kids can't open. If the worst sin I commit in life is having too much maple syrup in my tea, so be it. But as Eugene O'Neill once intimated the past and the future are the present. I instruct myself again to try to remember the happiness not the loneliness of that house I came from, and to take baby step tasks to try to help people--at least somebody. I must remember brains are organs as well as hearts, and, they, too, often need repair.

The Maine of My Youth

was dark.
It had no light.
The waves lapped broken
bits of beach glass on the shore.
They seemed like me.

Inside Rain

I don't want to end like you—a hole in the ground in an unmarked grave. I learned on my own that willingness and direction toward usefulness can be as strong as self-destruction. We can "watch the clock or seize the moment." I've dredged through muddy fields from the log cabin in Maine where I was trained to be a volcano. In my grandmother's house in Boston with the polished silver and Wedgwood plates, I was made to feel as small and unimportant inside as a kernel of corn. She couldn't drip a drop of endearment. There was no routine in life—just ups, just downs. Father was a drunk—I a bottler-upper. But somehow the spark of aliveness survived like the candle that continues to burn even when a blast of chill comes in from the window. Let this moth be. Let me be my own work of art in life. Let me channel this childhood anger away from myself so that sorrow's not permanently sealed.

In the State Hospital

Alone in the hallway,
writhing
on the cold, wet floor
my tattered pajama bottoms
are too long.

Prettiest Apple

So what if Christmas candles languish in July windows, so what if the pine tree still rests in the pile in the woods. So what if I don't take time to wash floors every day. Who cares if I don't fold underwear but throw it in a bin? So what if I want to suffocate those vegetables I hate, throw that ugly prom dress in the garbage and throw away the blouse whose button has fallen to the ground. I'm in a hurry. Let me be. I choke on triviality. As I once said, "I'm here for constant action." This thing called time, this constant pain hasn't healed by your recipe of whipping, cajoling and tormenting me. The lonely grape on the saucer was me. The constant cold I feel inside, the chronic rain doesn't cease. I keep repeating to myself, "Get up right now. It's time to do." Get out of your own way. Pick up the can you kicked across the lawn. Place it in the waste container. Give me oars and a rowboat, or paddles and a canoe to get to my self-willed destination. Keep by my side forever, friend. I've stopped the trembling inside, won't allow inner tears to bleed through. I've scorned sorrow's fugue, tried to erase the blue. Let me be in Venice on the first of May, be welcomed by a gondolier holding out a blazing lantern. Let me not be the rotten seed that has sown, but an ocean, not a mere sink full, of love. Allow me to be the prettiest apple in the bowl. Let me have peace and quiet within my soul.

I Want to Be …

A vision of light not dark,
the gold at the end of a rainbow,
the supporting block in a stonewall,
a fighter for life until the last petal falls,
a compulsive gambler for love,
a life that's led without bigotry,
a wind that roars through the trees,
a sparrow singing on a maple branch,
a constant flame,
a voice that booms across the world
        to lend a hand to the insane.

Outside St. Shepherd's Church — 1869

Someone threw a brick tear-
ing my shoulder blade.
I'm hope-
less, hurt, horrified,
and homeless.

Freezing

Believing
lunatics can't
feel the cold,
they amputated
both my feet.

My Fog Over the Harbor

Before I do it, I want you to know:

It's not your fault. It's not your fault. It's not your fault. It's not your fault.

Please, each day, light two candles, remember me and then blow one out. The one that glows and remains represents you, my survivor. Use intelligence. Put one foot in front of the other. I know you've inherited my mess but realize "like doesn't have to beget like," so don't disappear into an emotional cave. Keep me alive in your conversations; don't stick your head in the sand. Use your voice for those who don't have one. Remember 90% of people have some combination of mental illness in their families. You are not alone.

Most of all know: I want you to make it through and I want you to say each day:

It's not my fault. It's not my fault. It's not my fault. It's not my fault. It's not my fault.

And Then It Rained

Turning the kaleidoscope she saw splintered, then woven together, clicking, clinking chips of green, white, purple and then red glass. Click, click, crash goes the interior of the tunneled-like Rorschach inkblot. It ends with an always returning blue stone in the center. She tries with each twist to make the blue disappear but it keeps coming back. She's the person who never cried, the in-your-face one, the I-don't-care, the you're-stupid, the get-out-of-my-way, the I'm-in-a-hurry-dame, the you're-not-talking-fast-enough, the I'm-more-important-than-you, the what's-your-problem, sissy-cake, the potty-mouthed, the step-aside, you're-boring-me one, the non-respecter, the no-one-can-ever-hurt-me in a relationship again, the kicker of stones in her path, the one whose co-worker described as having "attitude," the one whose bumper sticker read "Bitch," the one who stabbed herself to death with a steak knife.

II

Margaret Bourke-White

(1904 –1971)

Don't Touch

My mother was emptying out the china closet in preparation for a holiday meal. Beautiful cherished dishes were placed on a white tablecloth on top of a wooden antique table. Dozens and dozens of dishes were there. I was angry—maybe at my sister, maybe at my mother. I don't even know why. I yanked on the end of the cloth and dishes crashed to the floor and broke into smithereens. To this day the most shocking thing to me is that my mother never became angry. If this had happened to me I might have thrown the kid against the wall. But not her. She quietly asked me what the matter was. In my mind I photographed myself feeling horribly guilty. But I never apologized. I'll say it now: "I'm sorry, so very sorry."

When You and I Were Young, You...

took ballroom dance at the Ritz; a neighborhood kid taught me
    to jitterbug.
were driven by your chauffeur to Driver's Ed; dad taught me
    on icy back roads.
played tennis on grassy courts; I snuck onto the Yale courts. No one
    watched or clapped.
spent summers where John Gunther lived; I babysat every day,
    earned $12.00 a week.
skied in winter at St. Moritz, I tried my cousin's worn-out skis
    in the park.
sat in front-row seats at the football stadium. I heard crowds
    roar from across the way.
attended mass every Sunday. I stayed at home, cooked the big meal
    for everyone.
listened to Mozart at symphony hall; I danced to jukeboxes
    in downtown soda joints.
soared from the diving board in a gas orange suit; I gulped gin
    in deserted bars for courage.

Klepto

I was at the oak-polished table in the Michigan State library and decided to go outside for a cigarette to take a break from studying geology. I left a dozen different types of rocks on the table along with my semester notes. Twenty minutes later when I returned, my notes and rocks were missing. I was stymied. A friend down the hall in the dorm missed a necklace given to her at high school graduation. More things disappeared: a book, a ring, a brass candlestick from the entrance table. This went on for months. One night at eleven o'clock, I noticed lights on in the basement storage room. No one was supposed to enter the area without permission, but I had to go down to pick up an important letter. Something seemed fishy. I told the "Dorm mother" so she began to discreetly keep an eye on "basement activities." Sure enough, we found out, Susan, I forget her last name, (lucky for her), was going down there, night after night, to "stash her treasures." When finally confronted, it turned out her trunk and suitcases held all the stolen items. Susan was from one of Philadelphia's wealthiest families. I did get my notes and rocks back, but it was too late. By that time, I had already taken up ornithology. The kleptomaniac was kicked out of school, never to return.

A Favorite Subject, Ralph

My brother is a do-doer, a diplomat in rags,
a hymn, a bullet with a song, a tortoise when he
wants to be, and then sometimes a snake. He's a
rat, a baby duck, a sparrow, as they say. When
I deserve it, he's a kudos-giver, a teaching Bible,
my own silver star.

Zoom

Do I want to photograph the outside, the side effects, the side he was on, the softer side, the better side, the left side, the right side, up-side down, the far side, side to side, the dark side, the wrong side, the playful side, the East side, the West side, this side, that side, the private side, the lighter side, the flipside, the public side of heaven? No. I want to portray what's on the *inside* of Gandhi.

The Wedding Ring

Attorney Black calls, informs me: "The court case is over. You're free." I slide off my ring; my finger seems sticky. A pale white non-tanned line remains. First comes tentative peace. But am I in the lost or the found? Wind blows the screen door open then it shuts with a slam. Music barrels from a neighbor's yard, then it stops. I feel sick to my stomach. I scream. Then sob. Then stop.

Shoot

Next to the yellow crime scene tape, one man, seven women, and nine children wait for the school bus. I feel like the clothes in my closet—dark. I frame them all, shoot in all directions.

USA, 1930's, Begonia

The sharecropper's daughter
attends school,
trading one ragged coat
and one pair of shoes
on alternate days
with her twin sister.

Buchenwald Fairy Tale, 1945

We didn't know. We didn't know. We didn't know.
We didn't know. We didn't know.

I photograph ribs.
Bodies on top of bodies on top of bodies on top of bodies on top of bodies.
All dead.
Most naked.
Some with curled toes.
Some in fetal positions.
Some with open mouths.

Leipzig-Mochau, 1945

In a slave labor camp inmates were sprayed in their mess hall with burning acetate. As they ran from the hall, they were machine gunned down by the Nazis. Men, scalded then shot, died with their feet pointing eerily toward the sky, legs in the air, like dead dogs.

Photographing Joseph Stalin for "Life Magazine"

Pock-marked,
without medals,
shorter,
fatter than me,
I shoot him.
Flash bulbs spill
on the floor
like bullet casings.
He laughs.

Beyond the Glam

Off in the corner beyond the glam of the yellow lotus
an injured wren huddles against the pine.
Four crows surround, then one goes in for the kill.
The wren flops on the granite, gasps, escapes.
I serve it water in an ochre saucer,
golden flaxseed in a vibrant bowl.
When I return later with my camera,
the wren is gone.
A crow caws, "So what."

The Jump

You'll miss barbecues on charcoal grills, sailboat rides on catamarans, the sounds of a tractor singing in a nearby field, a lawnmower purring down the street. You'll never see a graceful lemon leaf fall from its tree like the one I saw this morning. It made not a sound as I photographed a final tango on its way to earth. Its grave, the ground, grew prettier.

I'll never see you again in sassy shorts and Speedo bra, with wind-blown hair and salmon sneakers. Your end in life is like a root canal gone astray whose pain is never cured. Pine cones, when first fallen are green but you were as black as three day old road kill, a domino already fallen. You are dead. In my stupor, I photograph any truth I see.

Once Upon

I had one husband,
then another.
Both are gone.
Now I love
an Army Lieutenant
and he disappears.
I'm done.

Mother

I see in front of me a hand-carved figurine of you and Dad at your wedding. You're holding a bouquet of pink roses; Dad holds you. Your veil carries the shade of the roses on its crown. You looked as lovely the last time I saw you as on your wedding day, had the same joie de vivre to the end, even on the day before you had your fatal heart attack you were readying yourself to take your first airplane jaunt. Mom, it was you who set me on the path of realization that to fully understand one another we must be familiar with each other's life journeys, their hills, their valleys, their crevices in between. I think often of when you and Dad and I sat up all night to watch the incubation process of a preying mantis. You taught me it's okay to rest on my elbows sometimes and not feel guilty about it. You taught me if goals go astray to remember it's not over 'til you're dust. I learned to feed the pigeons because no one else would. Thanks for finding loveliness in some of my faults, encouraging me to be my own person. As Frida Kahlo once said, "You brought life and warmth to any place."

Bourke-White at Sixtyish

I realize you don't arrive until you get there. With boots on the ground, doves in my birdbath, rice without rocks in it, a paddle, an "Old Town" for the nearby lake, onward I'll go until it is over. With wafting white hair, we can, even at sixty, change tides like moons. The angler angles, marksmen mark, foragers forage, woodcutters cut wood, barkers bark, songsters sing, writers write, conductors conduct, educators educate. Photographers shoot straight down life's path. Through the truth-lens of my camera, life cannot lie. In my sometimes twisted stupor over content, I must pass to the world what I see.

III

Greta Garbo

(1905–1990)

Dear Mother,

I just passed the glass kitchen cabinets and noticed the darling bone china thimble made in England with blue and pink flowers budding out from the branch. Do you remember this is the one you gave me when I was nine? It's sitting next to the pewter-pear ice-cream mold you gave me when I left Stockholm. The beautiful small green Karl Laib clock Dad left me made the trip safely although I still haven't found a repairman to make it tick.

Sorry I haven't written sooner. I have been working 12-hour days from 7 in the morning until 7 at night. Then I go home and prepare vegetables and salad for supper. They still have me trying to lose weight. I've had my buck teeth fixed. (That's what they call teeth that stick out in front in the U.S.) Wish you could see them and let me know what you think. Sometimes I have two glasses of alcohol at night too. But that's all, Mom, so don't worry. How are the handmade papier mâché bunnies you made me for Easter faring? Hope they are in a safe place so they won't get destroyed. I miss them so. And don't let Sven near them! I want them for my children if I ever have any.

I'm so upset about some of the people in this country. Everything I do is published all over the world. I kissed one man and it was all over the newspapers that I had chapped lips. That jealous Marlene Dietrich had the gall to say that I had dirty underwear. It's unbelievable. No privacy, nothing is sacred. People wonder why I am standoffish. I just get so fed-up with this type of behavior. Someone told me it comes with the territory. Believe me, the thought has often crossed my mind to come home. But it would probably be like this at home too.

I miss you with all my heart.

Love,
Greta

Churchill, Onassis, Garbo

Is the story true? No one I know knows.
Sir Winston and Greta went sailing on Ari O's yacht.
Is the story true? No one I know knows.
For those of you reading, here's how it goes:
Sir Winston wanted to see Garbo's breasts, her naked toes.
Puerile fixations for such an old big shot.
Is the story true? No one I know knows.
Winnie tore Greta's dress, snatched her shoes on Ari's yacht.

Abortion Hollywood Style

Where is the fertile seed once plucked from me?
Among northern twinflowers adorning Swedish soil?
Among the cooing doves in weeping trees?
Where is the fertile seed once plucked from me?
With discarded flowers bobbing in the bluish sea?
In the killing fields sown with embryonic spoils?
Where is the fertile seed once plucked from me?
In the crimson fields of accidents and toil?

Dear Dad,

You've been gone for so many years now but every once in a while I get stopped in my tracks realizing how much I miss you. You'd never recognize me. I'm an actress now and have made a number of pretty good movies. In one of them, the character I play states she's "slowly opening her petals, becoming a woman of the world." I thought of you when I first read those lines. They represent some of what has become me since you died at the age of 48. But all of my lack of self-confidence, my Nordic standoffishness, my unwillingness to allow others to waste my precious time, my inability to not be frugal in spite of all the money I make, still exist within me. You would be proud that in spite of all this money, I carry my poles and skis home after a day on the slopes. I polish my leather shoes myself. I'm in bed by nine each night. Every so often I go to the neighborhood Lutheran Church to congregate with and speak Swedish with some of the parishioners. It's a group of good down to earth people. But usually I feel alone in spite of the many crowd groupings in my life.

Of course, I also think of the bad times. I will never be able to censor the nightmares of your alcoholism and the constant torment it brought to our family. But I know that whatever sadness and anger it brought us, you, too, bore shame for your agonizing behavior. I remember what you used to say, "If life hands you lemons, make lemonade." I didn't eulogize you at your funeral. But if I had I would have summed you up in two words: A Giver. I remember when you gave up your supper each night so your children wouldn't go hungry. That said it all to me. I believe you've finally found in death the peace you rarely had in life. Just wanted you to know I'm thinking of you.

Someday we'll meet again.

Yours,
Greta

Some Coffee, a Wooden Bench

Think I'll go up the street, pass the Catholic Church, meander up to the zoo to see the monkeys and the newborn llama. To there and back to where I'm staying at Jackie Gilbert's in the Hills should put a dent into today's walking goal. I need this, need to escape the maid and her chatter for several hours. Perhaps I'll drop by the Hollywood coffee shop before I trot full-speed ahead. Hopefully, that photographer who has been following me forever has a hangnail today and will leave me to my own devices. Perhaps the world will give me a few hours of privacy this morning. Good grief, don't they have anything else to do with their lives other than follow me around and watch each and everything I do. I can't even go into a bathroom. I come out to wash my hands and there's someone in my face with an autograph request. Don't people know yet that they can kiss my words in cinematic plots but not my lips? I want people to stay out of my killing fields. Hell, to me, is other people as Sartre says. Perhaps I should follow my dream to go home to Stockholm. But they would hound me there too. I'm almost to the park, so glad I got out of the rocking chair this morning. I wish the environs had a garden of Camellias. Oh no, I have to put a tissue in front of my face so that imbecile with the camera, the one who makes me toxic, won't get a good shot. At least the wooden bench in front of the monkeys is empty and all mine.

Greta on Amies

My goats and kittens made better friends than the ones I found in Paris.

For My Sister Alva

I'm like an empty acorn fallen from its tree.
News came from overseas; I couldn't be by your side.
My "twin," my "little sister," you barely had a chance.
You were my nutrient, my mineral, my laughter vitamin
in our life of boiling stew. You were my *middag* fellow
walker, well of sparkling water, my simple garden filled
with daisies in the spring. You were my childhood confidant,
my protector through life's rains, my co-lover of Arsta Inlet,
in the country, where we cooked the fish we caught over
a wooden fire, where we hunted for that fox with bows
and arrows we made out of fallen branches from that maple tree
so high. What would we really have done if it had crossed our path?
You were the wafting sea grass in a summer breeze, the golden
thread of sunlight in a darkened room. Your death stings me
each day. Only twenty-two years old in the morning of your life,
choked by vile tuberculosis. How could any so-called god
have done this to you, to us?

Waste Not, Want Not…

In a hotel hallway, Greta swipes leftover rolls
from another's breakfast tray, wraps them
in a napkin, hides them in
her blouse.
Later, she feeds them to
magpies and squirrels
in the Black Forest.

Would I Rather...

have men ogle me or not look at me at all? The problem is I'm a movie actress so, in reality, it goes with the territory. It's said I'm naturally erotic in my films. If I didn't like the idea, I never should have entered the profession in the first place. But I'm funny this way. While on the one hand, when I'm on screen, I suspect, both men and women ogle me. I'm seen through the "all-gender" lens. I've gone to the movies incognito and watched many viewers look me up, down and sideways and up, down and sideways again. Point is, it's expected. If you're a movie star people will examine you from head to foot and this I understand and have to tolerate. While this success in some ways can be a depressant, it truly is something I can and have to live with. Herein lays the problem. It's when I'm away from the job and off duty that I'm most annoyed when people ogle me. I bought a 1,000 acre farm in Sweden to get some privacy in life. Being Swedish and having been brought up in the tradition of people swimming in the nude, I was shocked when some of my servants in New York City actually charged voyeuristic neighbors to come and, unknown to me, watch me swim naked in my own pool. The world thinks it owns me. I can't even go to the bathroom at the Ritz without having someone banging on the door and asking me for an autograph. When I am off the job, I want to be an unobserved chicken in the barnyard coop, a tortoise in its shell, a mollusk. I don't live through you, don't gawk at you through open windows, and don't say if I think you have ugly furniture. No one tries to know the interior me. So leave me alone, world. I have rights. Don't tread on them. Put yourself in my position and take a hike!

To Moje

Greta's director and friend

When autumn leaves scatter from the maples into glens
when seagulls banter near the shores,
when someone serves little pony *cupsaken* (cupcakes) in July,
when horse-drawn sleighs pass by my front door,
I brood for you, I brood for you.

I Wondered If...

I would survive if I had no one to kiss on New Year's Eve. I sat with my two pets, Laurel and Hardy, in my lap and fed them each a treat. They kissed me after they ate them. Sweet! Then I put on an old movie and kissed the main actress, me, and told her it was a job well done. I wiped the screen of any trace of my kiss. By 12:01 I was in bed. I called Moje before I turned out the lights to wish him Happy 1935. No one was home. I switched off the lamp, hugged my pillow and was asleep in no time.

Outside Greta's Flat

There's a garden filled with coral roses,
beds of strawberries she once raised for sale,
blossomed cherry trees with vibrant pink noses,
a garden filled with broken-stemmed roses.
Planted fig tree fruit, near the iron gate, failed.
Daffodils bloomed by the fountain, paled.
The garden's filled with decaying coral roses.
And she once brought to market fresh berries for sale.

God Jul

At sixty-seven-years-of-holding-it-in, after the house
being filled with red tulips on Julafton (Christmas Eve),
after serving Jul Skinta (Christmas Ham), sweet and sour
red cabbage, gingerbread biscuits and jul grot, a porridge
with a hidden almond, good luck to the one who finds it
in their portion, after the emptied house, I'm in the third week
of a viral infection which has included fevers, chills, sore throat,
earaches and throwing up. I'm on the second go-round of an
antibiotic, this time 500 MG's of cefprozil. I wake up and vomit
in the bathroom sink again and then the toilet. I start crying,
then bawling. "I want my mommy, I want my mommy."

I'm a Let-It-Snow-Again Norsewoman

Let me wash my face with snowballs, use sparkling brook water to rinse.
I want no words with strangers but to picnic with friends
in the height of winter under orange trees near the trails.
I'll run naked in the snow in front of the old men
gazing from perched rocking chairs inside their mountain condos.
Then you'll know, even when I appeared frigid,
I was always warm within my heart.

Mata Hari

Frida Kahlo once said, "Make love, take a bath,
make love again."

I said, "Take two bites of the apple, do it right
and do it twice,"
as I followed espionage orders during WWI.

In the end, as I walk toward the firing squad I
know this will be my last lonely sunset.
In life we must all fall asleep.

A colony of bats fly in a rowing motion through
shutters of the prison's clock tower.

I remember what else Kahlo said,
"I hope the exit is joyful
and I never return."

IV

Edith Piaf

(1915 –1963)

From the Refrigerator...

of my mother's womb, I was an accident,
no right or wrong street address,
no birthing room, no robin's nest,
born right on the sidewalk.

Waiting for Her Again

I'm sitting in the square: No food, no drink, no mother's body next to mine as I wile away the hours, listening to her sing for money, waiting for her to once again drag me to the closest bar. There is no safe house in my life, only walls of sadness, notes of hate, ballads of rejection. Anger seeds like cancer within my soul. I never want to wait for her again, but I keep waiting. In my mind, I smash each shot glass, wine glass, gin bottle and tumbler under foot and pound them into the ground and then ping…remold each shard into a sparkling faerie of the alleys.

L'argent

> "I'm going to the top. I've always known it."
> Edith Piaf character in *La Vie en Rose*.

From the days when I sat with other homeless children on the curbs of our neighborhood, to the day when 2,000,000 people attended a memorial tribute to me in the Paris square where my mother once sang for money, I knew I'd achieve my goals. Someone once raised the question, "Whose child is she?" Another answered, "Nobody's." I had no sterling silver rattles, no piggy banks, nor silver fillings. There was no silver spoon in my mouth, no tinsel on the tree, no tree, no sequins on pretty party dresses, no party dresses or birthday parties. I did learn to knit with a pair of cold, damselfly, silver-plated needles in the Square where hungry mosquitoes boasted silver wings.

Balloons

I sat on the sidewalk curb in rags, my hair never washed and all skin filthy. Alone, while mother sang, I watched as other children with clean hands and faces flew yellow, red and blue balloons toward pink clouds. I never owned a balloon as a child, never galloped on a carousel stallion, never had a ham and cheese sandwich on a beach blanket; never fed fawns at the zoos I never went to; never paddled boats around ponds; never captained one.

All grown up now, I go to a shoe sale in Paris, fill the back seat of my car with fifty slippers. Each pair comes with a free balloon.

Monkey-See, Monkey-Do

In the mirror in the back of my mind I reflect her, ma mère. She sang on the street; I sang on the street. She had a temper; I have a temper. She tried and failed; I tried and failed but I tried again and again and won. We each fought our battles, our demons. She loved men as did I. I'm the monkey who saw and had the fortuity to do. Once I did, I fed myself pearls, autos, safaris and cruises to Casablanca. But nothing ever sated the emptiness mom caused by abandoning me.

My Little Sparrow

Dear daughter Marcelle,
when meningitis
claimed you
at only two and a half,
I was compelled
to prostitute
to pay for your little coffin.

Instead,
a man
offered me
ten francs
out of kindness.

Marcel, My Prizefighter

With you I drew a map of love, fought my demons.
I covered your left ankle with mine, tasted your salt before and after.
You made all harshness disappear. Now alone, with my heart
in critical care, all numbness, my thoughts join you
in death's homeland, stoop before the blackened moon,
where there are clouds, only clouds,
clouds and rain.

Hear My Song

All my life I've wanted to be in sync with the happy
inward me, to concentrate on what I had, not on what
I didn't have, to find my truth, express it.
This is the song I've always wanted to sing
and now can sing all because of him:
Je ne regrette rien.

Blueberry in the Needle

The needle is stashed under my quilt in my bedroom along with the shot of morphine I paid one million francs for to one of the leeches who preys on me. My apartment is filled with creeps, bats, insects, worms lurching in every corner. My life paints black. This morning the hypodermic needle looked like it had a blueberry stashed in its base. *Dieu*, did I hallucinate? But I'm not worried. I detest blueberries and it is my last shot. I won't need one again. I'm done. It's over. No more, the end, the finality, the postlude, termination, closure, by the wayside, thrown out, an old habit, passé compose. I'm finished.

A Toast for Marguerite Monnot

To the child prodigy at our table: white your plate, as is your soul, you resonate the tempo of a September day. You have no pillows under your elbows, you are the cherished lamb in my foal, the gentle bear that never needs to be declawed. You're the hardwood fire's warm spark in the wintered room, a spoonful of peace in my valleys. You bring love and loyalty with the strength of a granite bridge. You're like a butterfly that lights and then remains. You bring salt to my breadbox, cadence to my being, meaning to my song. To you, I dedicate this toast.

The Piaf Prescription

    (with a phrase from Sandra Cisneros)

Dare to sit *sadness on an elbow*.
Let life's notes scale toward the skies.
Pronounce the anthems of the autumn leaves.
Chant rhythmic melodies.
Score songs of life's symphonies and sadnesses,
then set them loose so you and I shall always live.

V

Carol Burnett

(1933 –)

February's Joyless Child

We move into a big complex on the hill. On
the shelf in the middle of one of the rooms sits
a book with "abandonment" in the title. Stark
white toilet seats are ice cold. I blow bangs
away from my eyes, need a haircut, a snack.
My mother never holds my hand when I walk
down the long, dark hallway. Dad works another
night shift. *God doesn't pay for the coal.*
No one claps when I memorize a long poem.

Childhood Scents

Dad, I remember in the sanatorium, the last time I saw you, when you had tuberculosis. My mask smelled of salty tears. Gloves I wore smelled of Johnson's Baby Powder. Metal carts reeked of alcohol, this time not on your breath.

And you, Mom, that old familiar smell *was there* the last time I saw you. We sat quietly next to each other, so Nanny wouldn't hear us discussing plans for me to take my step-sister Chrissy to NYC to live with Don and me. For you alcohol was a constant companion, a shampoo at the beauty parlor, an I'm a downer in the morning-pick me upper, a let me sing enchantress, a make me happy for awhile great pretender that helped you get through long afternoons by spilling itself into your lonely mouth.

My Shoebox

Nanny, you were my polished Mary Jane's,
my shine, my effervescent glow.
You kept me clear of life's heels, gave me cleats
in the snow. You loosened the knots.
Guided by your footprints, I stepped forward
with my strong, leather soul, nearly graceful
in this ballet called life.

On the Train

I miss San Antonio. It was so lovely and peaceful there. From this train window we pass old stonewalls, budding trees in spring, green grass getting ready. Thank goodness—notice I didn't say thank the lord—there haven't been any St. Christopher statues in any of the passing yards. They would have been an interruption to nature's beauty. I was brought up that when you saw his statue you thought Catholics probably lived there. I think it was suggested they were beneath, below us. We were supposedly the upper class. It wasn't said out loud but insinuated. I'd see a little statue on a dashboard and sometimes snicker to myself. But I haven't seen any lately or maybe I'm not looking at people's dashboards but have learned to look into people's eyes and trustingly into their souls. I read an article that said "St. Christopher never existed." I'm a young girl but already realize that it's what the person driving the car behind the statue believes that matters.

At the Welfare Dentist

One by one
drilling
and drilling
each of nine
teeth,
filling
cavities
without any
Novocain
to kill the pain.

Going to the Movies

Nanny and I escaped our two-by-four apartment to the early shows to save money. In the theater, I'd hope each show would last forever, become married in spirit to them. I carried my dreams up the street, housed in my heart, took them to the couch with me each night, hid them under pillows and resurrected them each morning. I knew I wanted to be great on the stage at UCLA, on Broadway, on TV. I got outside the self, became someone I wasn't, made people laugh and howl, forgot all about my bucked teeth.

Mom, Down the Hall Again

sleeping it off on top of the covers. You once said, "A beautiful day doesn't depend on the weather." How would I know? I am alone again in front of the kitchen sink, performing your job as a mother. I squeeze the near-empty jar of Jergen's, wish you were here to soothe me at least once in awhile, instead of sliding into constant selfishness. I need you to smooth the bumps, heal my chapped hands, be the lotion that makes my world glide, bring softness back to your baby.

Don, You Were My...

eye of the needle,
ice cream in the cone,
softball in the glove.

honey in Earl Grey tea,
sugar in the cotton candy,
bouquet in the cream-colored bowl,

Scrabble triple word score,
poem in the typewriter,
kitten with front paw in its saucer,

onyx ink in the fountain pen,
fire in the woodstove,
comforter, always my comforter.

"Blame It on My Youth"

*Recorded on the Carol Burnett Show,
volume 6, 1974 by Bernadette Peters*

It happened more than two decades ago when Don and I were in the process of ending our marriage... He pulled up in a Gray Chevrolet with G5000 on its license plates, was in his police blue outfit. I hid behind the side door. He slammed an envelope on the porch, quickly returned to his "Mr. Important" car, then screeched out of the driveway. The return address on the smeared envelope read, "New York City District Court." My presence was requested, thirty days from the date on the summons, my ordered invitation to attend the demise of it all, crying time again.

As I lip-synched the Bernadette Peters song on my way across the room to telephone the news to my sister, the music came to an abrupt end.

We Were

timeless,
seamless,
ageless,
fearless,
...never
aimless,
tireless,
pointless,
deathless,
or so I thought.

On the Cover

I've finally made it, photographs of me on the dust cover of the autobiography penned by me, "One more Time". When I look back I'm astonished I've treaded this far in life, from a one-room apartment (Room 102 in Hollywood) to the cover of my second book. When I think of how I felt growing up, it's amazing—both my mom and dad were consumed with what I call liquid courage. It controlled them, broke them and could have broken me. How did I become what I've become? Who threw away the x-ray of my broken heart? Who put the "sun" in Sunday, the "wonder" into wondrous, the "glo" into glorious, the "on" in one? Who took the "blu" out of blue, the "no" out of nowhere and no one? Who forced me to use a polished silver creamer on a rainy day? Who makes the difference in life between the morning shower and the evening prayer? Who will have made the difference between the birth canal and the old pine casket? Who has irrevocably charged and changed my life? I yell, I scream, I screech, I chant, the answer is *me*.

Carol's Motto

Walk as quickly at 6 pm as at 6 am.

Defense Against Being a Workaholic

I can't take on the world, deal with all the sorrow, widespread slaughter, can't comfort every dying child whose life force spilled over red dandelions on his/her final day. I can take comfort in the outdoors on a fifty-degree day pulling weeds (and allaying my guilt over taking time off from the studio). I sit on my metal chair, purchased at the antique shop down the street; allow a good sailing breeze to brush against my cheeks. I will not allow the devil to make me deal with all his triumphs. I will not listen to people who blame their mothers or fathers for their miserable lives. If gog's—did I say gog? I meant god's shiny locomotive runs me down, don't blame it on the engineer, I will be to blame. I was, in my own way, on a track where I shouldn't have been. If I can't enjoy the tinkling of the shade against the sill, the setting of the sun against the ocean, then I'll not be able to deal with a world without happiness, if it arrives. I must follow my instincts… the way to joy.

Carrie

I do what love shouldn't have to do—invade your privacy. I mistrust you, your classmates, even the principal of your private school. I've made your "friends" leave their handbags on the kitchen table to prevent them from delivering drugs to your bedroom. You're giving me, your mother, repeat lessons on how a person can ruin her life. My mother's boundary trespasses, that I thought I had finally fenced, have been crossed again with you.

Back Home in San Antonio Forty Years Later

An old, blind man opens the door.
The hallway paint is chipped.
My roller skating marks
remain.

Carol's Theory

What we all
need
woven
deep down
into the fabric
of our souls
is
laughter.

About the Author

Martha Deborah Hall's poems appear in numerous national journals including, *Bellowing Ark*, *Common Ground Review*, *Las Cruces*, *Old Red Kimono*, *Tale Spinners*, *Tapestries*, *The Poet's Touchstone* and *Watch the Eye*. She is the winner of the 2005 John and Miriam Morris Chapbook contest for her collection *Abandoned Gardens*. She was a semi-finalist in the 2007 Concrete Wolf Chapbook contest. Plain View Press published two previous books, *Two Grains in Time* and *My Side of the Street in 2009*. Also, in 2009, Hall was honored by the New Hampshire Poet Laureate to be one of NH's featured poets. Her Chapbook *The Garbo Reels* has recently been published by Pudding House Publications. Hall is a member of the Academy of American Poets. She is a past President of the Amherst Junior Women's Club. Hall holds degrees from Ohio Wesleyan and Columbia University and is currently a real estate broker with Coldwell Banker in Amherst, New Hampshire. Copies of Hall's books may be purchased through Plain View Press, The Toad Stool Book Stores, Border's, Barnes and Noble or Amazon.com.

www.ingramcontent.com/pod-product-compliance
Lightning Source LLC
Chambersburg PA
CBHW052110070526
44584CB00017B/2421